The

Little Book

of

Missing Money

2nd edition

MARY PITMAN

WELCOME!

I know you want to get right into how to search for and find money on www.missingmoney.com or www.unclaimed.org and the other sites I recommend. Good luck on your treasure hunt! Email your success stories to themissingmoneylady@gmail.com and I'll post them on www.TheLittleBookOfMissingMoney.com. Inspire others!

Follow me on Twitter at MaryFindsMoney for updates as they become available. Or "Like" missingmoneybook on Facebook, where I post information about deadlines for filing and other missing money tidbits.

CONTENTS

PREFACE

Linda had a string of bad events happen to her. Her mother died. Ten months later her husband died. Then someone broke into her son's house and shot, but did not kill, his dog. Linda worked hard as an orthopedic nurse and also had a second job. I knew her because we worked together as RNs.

If anyone could use a break it was Linda.

I was working in the recovery room (where patients wake up from surgery) on a Saturday. They only keep one room going at a time on the weekend, so I had plenty of time between patients. I spent that time looking up friends, family and strangers on the missing money site.

I was actually looking up a doctor who had stopped by that day. He had the same last name as Linda. I entered the last name and city, and was surprised when Linda's name popped up. She had an unclaimed insurance policy, but no amount was listed.

Linda was off that day, but I promised myself that I'd give her the information the next time we worked together. On that day, I made small talk and finally got to the point.

"I have this hobby," I said. "I like to find money for people on the missing money site. And I found a listing for you."

She took the paper, looked at it, and then looked away. It was a combination of almost crying and being nearly speechless.

"Mary, I've been getting calls and letters from attorneys and firms saying that I had money but they all want a lot of money to help me get it," she explained. "I was determined to find this on my own, but I didn't know where to begin." She went on to say that one person wanted $700. Another wanted $2,100.

I was appalled that people would be forced to pay what I considered a ransom to get their own money. I assured her I would do everything I could to help her.

As I walked away, I realized she was not alone. There were many more people like her. That was the moment I decided to put all the search tips that I had discovered over the past several years, into a book.

Linda, in the meantime, did a basic search to see if she had other listings. She did. That inspired her to share the information about missing money with the other nurses on her floor. Many of them found money too.

Several weeks later, Linda called me from the post office. "Mary, I have checks in front of me for $63.50, $100, $55.84, and $2339.80. I've been out of work for three weeks. I fell and broke my arm in three places. I don't have insurance. I didn't know how I was going to pay my rent," she said, sobbing with relief.

Linda's four checks, totaling $2,559.14, came from a refund, a credit balance, a savings account and a group policy benefit.

In the search process, Linda discovered that her mother had American Express stock from her years as an employee there. The stock, valued at $7,200 when she found it, has since grown in value to $7,800. The finder's fee rose proportionately from $2,100 to $2,700.

By working with the transfer agent, she learned that she will only have to pay probate costs of $285 before the funds will be released.

My initial research for this book centered on individual state sites. I found multiple ways that names are recorded in these sites. The thing is, if you don't enter the name exactly as it is recorded, you will never find the listing. But take heart—there are an amazing number of ways to search.

I found additional sites beyond the state unclaimed property sites. Every time I found one, I thought "I should include this in my book but it doesn't fit with what I'm doing." When I tapped into unclaimed child support payments, I knew I had to rethink my initial concept for the book.

As I continued my research, I came across many questions people were asking and problems they were encountering in their search for unclaimed money. I decided to find the answers to those questions. This book is the result of that quest.

All of the sites I refer to are free to search and free to claim, just like the state sites. I do mention some fee-based services that will help you with specific issues. I am not affiliated with any of them; nor do I get referral fees. In fact, they don't know that I am including them in this book.

I hope you find lots of money, not only for yourself, but also for friends and family. When you start sharing this information, you'll understand the joy I get from helping people. There's nothing like it.

Happy treasure hunting!

Mary Pitman

THE TERMINOLOGY

There are four terms you need to be familiar with as you go through this book.

Escheat refers to items that have met the state inactivity period, generally about 3-5 years. The state then gets possession of them.

Pre-escheat is that period of time between the start of inactivity (or dormancy) to when it gets turned over to the state. It is when the items are the hardest (but not impossible) to find.

Holder refers to the company that has the money that needs to be turned over to the state.

Owner is the person to whom the money ultimately belongs.

FINDER'S FEES –
TO PAY OR NOT TO PAY

If you are contacted by someone who wants a finder's fee to put you in touch with your money, the first thing you should do is go to your state unclaimed property site and look for *free*. Go to **www.unclaimed.org** and click on your state. If you prefer to call or write, the contact information for each state is available on **www.unclaimed.org**, on **www.misingmoney.com** and in this book. There is no charge if the notification came from the state, except for Texas that charges 1.5% for claims above $100.

Most states limit what finders can charge. Finders may also be limited as to how soon they can approach you after a listing is posted. It can be as long as four years from when the state receives it. This is so you have a chance to find and claim it for free. These limitations only apply to listings on the state unclaimed property site. They do not apply to property in the pre-escheat phase—the period before it gets turned over to the state; or in the case of a listing that never gets turned over to the state.

I have included information about each state's finder's fee laws in the State Contact Information chapter. If you have questions about a letter you received, or a contract you signed, contact the state unclaimed property office or an attorney.

Some finders rely on you not knowing the state law. Be informed!

I have a friend who contacted me after receiving a letter from an attorney who wanted 1/3 of my friend's $10,000+ listing for his business. My friend got him down to $3,000 and felt I was missing out on a huge opportunity by not doing the same.

"You can make a lot of cash doing this," he said.

I explained that this goes against my core belief that people should not have to pay a ransom to get their own money. I directed him to the Illinois unclaimed property site. It took less than two minutes for him to find his listing.

Here's the thing: Illinois only permits a 10 percent finder's fee; plus the listing has to have been with the state for at least 24 months. Keep in mind the solicitation came from *an attorney*! He was based in Illinois so you would think he would respect the law in his own state.

Even if you don't intend to use one right now, record the contact information for each finder. Beware of this type of business if the only address is a P.O. Box. You don't have to respond immediately to the finder's pitch. Tell him you'll check everything out and get back to him.

Then Google the finder's name. Firms can have more than one Web site, marketing their services to both businesses and individuals. Don't be afraid to dig deep into their Web sites. You may find testimonials from holder companies (those companies that are holding the money) that can provide a valuable search clue, or information that will help you narrow your search.

The Illinois unclaimed property program has some wonderful information about finders. Go to **http://www.treasurer. il.gov/programs/cash-dash/protect-your-money.aspx** for details.

The Vermont unclaimed property web site had another great tip: "Be wary of businesses that require you to sign non-disclosure or non-circumventing agreements that are designed to prevent you from independently verifying the identity of the people you are considering doing business with."

There is no time limit on when you can claim money that the state is holding for you—except that Indiana keeps the money after 25 years; and Idaho keeps it after 10 years. However, it is a common scare tactic to be told that you will lose your money if you don't respond right away. The money may be reaching the end of the pre-escheat phase. Pre-escheat is that time period between the last contact with the owner and the date when the money is to be turned over to the state. Once it gets turned over, it's much easier to find. It's to the finder's benefit to get you to grab the money in this pre-escheat phase.

Although they will not tell you what the listing is or where it is, ask the person who contacted you how long the account has been inactive. Then ask when it is schedule to get turned over to the state. This is necessary information so that you to make an informed decision. There's a big difference between waiting for something that will get turned over in two months vs. two years. If you are told the property will not be turned over to the state, that's a clue as to where to look.

Not everything gets turned over to the state. Some examples are:

- Federal listings such as IRS and HUD refunds

- City, county and state tax refunds

- Overages from tax sales or foreclosures

- Impact fees

These listings have time limits for when money can be claimed. In addition, the limitations placed on finders do not apply. Licensing requirements may also be waived.

Federal listings must be claimed through the agency that is holding the money. Check with your city or county treasurer if you think you may be due a tax refund.

If your home was foreclosed or you lost the property due to an inability to pay your taxes, any amount above what is owed is supposed to go to you. Most people are unaware of this. They don't think of giving the county or their mortgage lender their forwarding address. These listings can be substantial and are a favorite of finders. Check with the Clerk of Court, the county treasurer or tax office. Check with your mortgage lender to see if your foreclosed home sold for more than you owed on it.

Finding impact fees that should be refunded can be quite complex. Depending on the wording, the impact fees may get returned to the developer or to the current owner of the property. If the house has been foreclosed, it gets more complicated. There is often no list of these assets.

Finders may claim they can get the money for you faster than if you filed the claim on your own. Not true! As long as you follow the instructions for submitting the claim, yours will be put through at the same pace as the finder's. If you don't include everything the state asks for, then yes, your claim will be delayed.

Many states, such as Texas, require that the finder (or any other term they are using), be licensed and/or registered with the state and have a current sales tax permit.

Check with the unclaimed property division to verify that the finder is allowed to do business in your state. The rules may not apply if they are contacting you about pre-escheat listings or ones that never get turned over to the state.

Massachusetts not only requires their finders to register with the state, but also has a Conflict of Interest clause that states: "No heir finder shall be allowed to register with the Abandoned Property Division and represent the interests of owners if this person or entity performs pre-escheat due diligence work for a holder." [960CMR4.06(2)]

This means that there are companies that market their services to places like banks and brokerages. They help them identify dormant accounts and deceased owners. This is a good thing for property holders; it helps them comply with abandoned property laws.

The company that provides this service then searches for the owner of the property, using the information it gleaned for the holder. For a 35 percent or more finder's fee, they will connect the owner with the money due. Some search firms market their services to holder companies by advertising on their Web site that the search "is free to you with a reasonable cost to your investors." It is the holder's duty to perform due diligence—making an attempt to locate the owner. To meet that duty, the holder hires the locator firm. But the holder doesn't pay them. You do.

Hopefully the holding companies will start doing the right thing for their customers/clients and list, on their Web sites, the names of those in pre-escheatment, thus giving people a chance to get the full amount of their money before it gets turned over to the state. Many performing rights organizations for actors and musicians do this. If you can hold out, eventually the money will get turned over to the state in most cases.

If the information is about a deceased family member, go through old tax returns. Look for things like a 1099-DIV form that reports dividend income from stocks (you'll need to find the transfer agent, usually available through the company's Investor Relations section); or a 1099-INT form that reports interest which, in turn, would give you a clue about insurance policies, bank accounts or other investments.

Should you decide to use the business that contacted you know this: You will still have to provide the pertinent documents. If you are a legal heir, you will, in nearly every situation, have to provide a copy of your driver's license, the certified death certificate, and other documents such as a marriage license and/or birth certificate that prove your relationship. If there was a will or trust, you'll need to provide those documents also.

At that point, you've done most of the work. Are you sure you want to give up 35 percent or more? You can always hire someone later to help if you get stuck in the process.

Be aware that there are dozens of Web sites trying to get people to become a professional finder, touting how easy it is to make money. That's why it's important that you check out the firms that contact you. Some are legitimate...others aren't.

Consumer protection agencies warn that legitimate search firms do not require payment up front. Inner alarms should go off if someone asks you to pay first; or if the fee is not based on a percentage of the amount collected. All costs should be included in the fee. There should be no additional charges for attorney fees, court costs or anything else.

If you don't feel you are being treated fairly, try to resolve the problem by going up the chain of command at the company. If that fails, you can always file a complaint with the Better Business Bureau in the city where the search firm is located, your state attorney general or with the Federal Trade Commission. Above all, never *ever* pay for an online search.

FUN FACTS

Some banks, transfer agents, life insurance companies and even some states sell their unclaimed property information to finders for a fee.

AVOID MISSING MONEY SCAMS

Here are the top five red flags to alert you to a missing money scam:

1. **It comes as an email.** State unclaimed property offices will not use email to contact you. They simply don't have that information. It's too hard to verify that the email address is truly yours.

2. **It says it's from the National Association of Unclaimed Property Administrators.** NAUPA is a professional organization that the unclaimed property administrators belong to; much like a doctor belongs to the American Medical Association. NAUPA is not involved in reuniting people with missing money, just like you won't get your lab results from the AMA.

3. **You get referred to someone else**. The treasurer handles all claims through its own office. The work is never outsourced.

4. **You're asked for your bank account information**. Granted, in many cases you will have to supply your Social Security number on a form you submit, but NEVER your bank account info. There is no direct deposit with unclaimed property.

5. **There is a fee to file the claim.** This is false for all 50 states. Legitimate search firms even within the U.S. do not charge an upfront fee.

WHAT TO DO IF YOU GET ONE OF

THESE EMAILS

If you have questions about a contact you received, do not call the number listed. Look up your state unclaimed property office by going to the chapter in this book on State Contact Information; or go to **unclaimed.org** and click on your state; or go to **missingmoney.com** and click on the map of the US. Scroll down for the state contact info.

If it is found to be false, report it to the Internet Crime Complaint Center at **www.ic3.gov** and the Federal Trade Commission at **www.ftccomplaintadvisor.com**.

THE BASICS

Are you ready to start your treasure hunt? If you encounter confusion or get discouraged, remember this: *you are on a no-risk, win-win journey!* Be patient, follow the guidelines I've outlined, and enjoy the journey!

1. The best place to begin is at **www.unclaimed.org**. You can go directly to your state. Another source is **www.missingmoney.com**. Not all states participate. On the home page next to your name where it asks for your state, enter ZZ to search all participating states. This is good for a quick look, but don't stop here!

2. I get more hits by going directly to the individual states. There can be quite a lag time between when info appears on the state site and when they upload it to missing money. In addition, very old listings are dropped but remain on the state site. For Illinois, listings before 1992 are not on the state site. You have to call to have a search done.

   Click on the map of the United States on the missing-money.com home page. It will take you to a color-coded map. Green states have their information on the site. Blue do not. Check any state by clicking on it. Who administers the program varies by state. In Georgia, it's the Department of Revenue. In California, it's the

11

state comptroller. In Minnesota, it's the Department of Commerce. The link will take you to the right place. If you prefer to write or call, the addresses and phone numbers are listed below the map and in this book.

3. Claims must be filed in the state in which they are held.

4. You may have money in a state that you never lived in. According to escheat priority rules, the first priority goes to the state of the owner's last known address. If the owner or the owner's address is unknown, the money goes to the state of the holder's corporate headquarters.

5. What documentations you will need to submit depends on the type of claim you're making, and what the state requires. At a minimum, expect to send a copy of your driver's license. To get your money as quickly as possible, follow the requirements to the letter! If you omit anything, your claim will be delayed. Before you send your claim in you, consider calling the unclaimed property department to verify that you are enclosing everything they require.

6. Save your claim number so you can monitor the entire process. It will make your life much easier if you keep this number in a safe and easily accessible place. If you don't hear anything, it's up to *you* to follow up. The length of time it takes to get the money depends on whether or not there has been a lot of publicity about the missing money/unclaimed property program. If

you haven't heard back in a month, it's time to check your claim status.

7. Check for missing money *at least* once a year. Just because you did or did not find money once doesn't mean it won't be there the next time you look. National Find Your Missing Money Day is April 16, the day after you have to pay your taxes. However, you can check at any time.

FUN FACTS

The largest single payout to an individual in US history was $6,100,000 from a stock claim
to a woman in Missouri.

THE NAME GAME

8. The less you enter, the broader your search. You can enter as little as one letter in the Last Name box on missing money. That will get you a state and an address, or at least a city.

9. The more detail you add, such as middle initial or city, the narrower the search.

10. If your name has an unusual spelling, look under all versions. For example, Elisabeth could also be Elizabeth. My last name is Pitman with one "t." I always look under Pittman also because most people misspell my last name. If the address is correct and it was a company you did business with, then file the claim and explain that the error is on the holder end. The correct spelling of your name does not matter as much to others as it does to you.

11. If there are multiple common spellings of your name, look under all of them. For example: Deborah, Debra; John, Jon; Jean, Jeanne, Jeannie; Katherine, Kathryn, Catherine.

12. Look under the formal and informal versions of your name: Catherine, Cathy, Cathie; Robert, Rob, Robbie, Bob, Bobby; Richard, Dick, Rick; etc.

13. If your last name has an apostrophe or other punctuation, search with and without. (i.e. O'Leary, Oleary.) Some states accept the punctuation, others do not.

14. Varying punctuation and spaces can bring up additional listings.

15. If your last name is followed by Jr., Sr., Esq., II, III, IV etc, you would think that those designations would follow the name, right? Not necessarily. While some last name listings may be in that sequence, you can also enter just the ending in the Last Name box.

16. If you have a professional designation associated with your name such as MD, DO, DDS, DMD, DPM, DVM, RN, ARNP, CRNA or anything else, you can enter just that designation under Last Name and you will find listings.

17. Put Mr. or Mrs. (with a period and without) where it asks for the Last Name. The only sense I can make of this is that by putting Mr./Mrs. in the Last Name space, it then puts it at the beginning of the listing so it reads Mrs., John Doe instead of Doe, Mrs. John. The same is true for Spanish salutations: Sr. and Sra. Also check Mr and Mrs, Mr & Mrs, Miss, Ms, Dr. and Rev.

18. Reverse your name. Sometimes listings will be found with your last name first and your first name last.

19. Enter your first name only under the Last Name. It will bring up a state and address or city.

20. Enter your entire name (first last--like on an envelope) under Last Name.

21. Enter Unknown, Unclaimed, Moved or Illegible under Last Name. See if your address matches any of the listings.

22. Look up all names you have ever used in every state you lived in.

23. You may also have listings that are buried under a bank or brokerage listing. For example, you bank at Banks R Us. Its address is:

> Banks R Us
> FBO Jane Doe
> 123 Main St.
> Any town, USA

Since the first name on the address is the bank, that's what the listing is under. With your name as the next line, it gets put in the address slot and thus is unsearchable by name. This can also be the case with brokerages. (FBO = For the Benefit Of; also FAO = For the Account Of)

Think about banks you used previously. They may have been taken over by another company and the name has changed. However, the names are never changed for the listings on the unclaimed property site. For example, if you were a customer of First

Union, look under that name and see if there are any listings like the example above.

24. Enter FBO or FAO under the Last Name.

25. Money for trusts can be in unclaimed property limbo. Under Last Name enter: Trust; Irrevocable Trust; Revocable Trust; Rev Trust; Revoc Trust; Living Revocable; Living Trust; Trust Fund, Retirement Trust and Family Trust.. Trusts can also be listed under the date they were started as well as UDT, UTD, DTD, U/A, UA, FBO, ITF, TTEE, or Trustee.

26. Enter Safe Deposit under Last Name

27. For children's savings accounts, the person who opened the account is usually listed as a co-owner. Other ways to search include enter UGMA (Uniform Gift to Minors Act), UTMA (Uniform Transfer to Minors Act), Custodian, or ACF (as custodian for) under Last Name.

28. Don't forget to look up friends and family, including the dearly departed.

29. Speaking of the dearly departed, would you ever think to search using these terms? By now you know there is no limit how a person's money may be listed. If you're searching for money you may be entitled to from a deceased relative, enter these terms in the Last Name:

(The) Estate of	(The) Est of
Deceased	POD (Payable on death)
Trustee	Executor
Beneficiary	No Beneficiary
Unk Heir	Unknown Heir

30. Retirement listings can be found under Roth IRA (all under Last Name) and Last Name: Roth, First Name IRA. Yes, I know there are people named Ira Roth and they will show up. I found a listing for a woman's Roth IRA by searching as I described above. This was like the example in #23 where the next line was FBO with her name. It was lost forever if she only searched for her name. Also enter under Last Name: IRA, 401K, 403B, Pension or Profit Sharing. Check the chapter on Retirement Benefits for additional places to search.

31. If the listing is very old and you have to send proof that you lived at the address listed but don't have it, you can try:

County Tax collector	A church where you were a registered member
Utility company	
Voter Registration Office	A school your child attended
Driver License Office	Library, if you had a card
Employer	Insurance agent
Professional License	Mortgage company/Bank
Doctor's office records	Credit report—get yours free once a year from **www.annualcreditreport.com**
College transcript	

FUN FACTS
The oldest person in the nation to receive unclaimed property
is 102-year-old Zelma Fraley
of Barrackville, WV

CHARITIES AND CHURCHES

This is an especially important area given that the economy is so bad and donations to non-profit organizations that help the needy are down. Some of the listings can be decades old. And if they are from donors, then these people never got a thank you. Lack of one thank you might make contributors feel unappreciated, resulting in them sending their donations elsewhere. See additional tips under Businesses and Corporations that apply here.

32. Search as many variations of a charity name as possible. As an example, for The American Cancer Society under the Last Name on missingmoney.com or Business Name on the state site enter:

The American Cancer Society   American Cancer Society
American Cancer   Am Cancer Soc
ACS   Cancer Society
Relay for Life   Avon 3 Day
Avon 3 Day Race   Avon Breast Cancer Day
Avon Breast Cancer 3 Day   Breast Cancer 3 day
Breast Cancer Race for the   Breast Cancer Society
Cure

Now enter the following terms as I have designated:

FIRST NAME	LAST NAME
Avon B 3 Da	Cancer
American C	Society
American Canc	Society
American Cancer	Society
Cancer	Society
Society	American Cancer
Society	Cancer
Society Am	Cancer
Susan	Komen
Foundation	Komen

There are probably more. This gives a good illustration of how many (and often times inconceivable) variations of a name there can be. I didn't even break a sweat putting this list together!

Remember from #14 above that punctuation and spaces make a difference.

33. Look under the full name of the organization, but also search under the abbreviation it is known by. (e.g. American Heart Association, AHA.)

34. With churches, if part of the name is "Saint" also check "St"—with and without the period. If "First" is part of the name, look up 1st and 1. Shorten the name: Presbyterian, Presby; Methodist, Metho; etc.

FUN FACTS

The Texas unclaimed property site will let you donate your
unclaimed property to charity.

HOSPITALS

35. Look under the hospital's current name and any former name. Many hospitals have changed from XYZ Hospital to XYZ Medical Center.

36. If the hospital is affiliated with a university, look under all variations of the university name. Like the example in #23. When the mail is addressed to the university and the hospital is the second name on the address, the listing goes under the university name.

37. If the hospital is corporate owned, look under the corporation name.

38. With so many hospitals buying physician practices, don't forget to look under the physician's name for insurance payments.

39. Payments to doctors may also be listed under the practice name, i.e. Sandy Beaches Urology.

BUSINESSES AND CORPORATIONS

From mom and pop businesses to major corporations, this is where the big bucks are. The bigger the business, the more likely it is they have hundreds, if not thousands of listings. You'll never hear this story on TV because people don't care if businesses have money. But business owners and shareholders care.

40. On the missing money site where it asks for the Last Name, enter the name of a business.. Each state has a place to enter the name of a business. Let's use an example of a business that no longer exists: Bear Stearns based out of New York. So NY is where we'll start the search. The steps and tips in this example (#41-48) can be used in any other business search, just as they are presented here:

41. Do the obvious and enter the business name as it is known. If there are more than two words in the name, reverse the order. Under Business Name, enter: Stearns Bear. But wait! There's more!

42. Now enter it as an individual. Last Name: Stearns; First Name: Bear

43. Reverse that. Last Name: Bear; First Name: Stearns

44. Now put both names under the individual Last Name: Bear Stearns. Leave the First Name blank.

45. You guessed it! Reverse it by switching the names still leaving it under the individual Last Name: Stearns Bear. First Name is still blank.

46. Allow for typos such as Bear Sterns.

47. When there are two or more words in the name, eliminate the space between them: Bearstearns

48. Drop the last letter from the name. When people are typing the name quickly, the last letter can get dropped. If there are two or more names in the business, drop the last letter from each word individually. Bear Stearn, Bea Stearns.

49. If there are more than the maximum that the state will show, (California only shows the first 500 listings, North Carolina 250, Texas 200, etc.), work your way through the alphabet like this: ABC A; ABC B; ABC C and so on. Just because there is a limit on what will show, there is no limit on what you can claim if you know how to look. This will let you look up the maximum with each entry.

50. Under Last Name enter Co, Company, Corp, Corporation, Inc, LLC, Ltd.

51. Texas is the most user-friendly state when it comes to corporations or other large businesses. When you click on the search page, click on Search Tips on the left. At the very bottom, it gives you a number to call if you are

a business or a major corporation. This way, you don't have to file dozens or hundreds of individual claims.

52. Sometimes the account is listed as Store #123 or Store 123. There's even one where it spelled out the numbers—Store Forty One O Two in Texas. (Ring a bell with anyone?) When the address begins with the store number and then the name of the business follows, the listing goes under the first line of the address. (Refer to #23) In this case it's the store number.

53. Follow the corporate history and look up every company involved.

For example: May Dept. Stores became Federated Dept. Stores that took over Macy's. They are all there. This is an especially important concept when it comes to banks. All the banks that no longer exist such as Barnett Bank, First Union, South Trust, etc., have dormant money being held by the states. You can research bank "genealogy" by going to the National Information Center at **www.ffiec.gov/nicpubweb/nicweb/nichome.aspx**

Even businesses and banks that have gone under such as Circuit City, Linens 'n Things and too-big-to-fail-but-did Washington Mutual have listings. If you are one of the subordinated debt holders that filed a claim against these or other bankrupt/failed companies, then these listings are a good thing for you to be aware of and bring to the attention of the bankruptcy court. Check with the FDIC for Washington Mutual.

LOCAL, STATE AND FEDERAL GOVERNMENT

With property values dropping across the nation and, as a result, local services being cut due to a decreased tax base, unclaimed local, state and federal money is an important area to research. This is a part of the missing money story that never gets reported.

But first, let's talk about where you may have missing money with your local government.

54. Check with your county auditor or treasurer to see if you have a refund due from your taxes. These listings do not get turned over to the state and have a limited time to claim them.

55. If you lost your home because you couldn't pay your taxes and the tax lien/deed sold for more than you owed, you are entitled to the overage. Be sure the property tax office has an address where you can be reached.

56. The same holds true if your home was foreclosed. For example, if you owed $110,000 on your home, but the bank sold it for $150,000, the extra money is yours. Check with your mortgage lender. If the home hasn't sold yet, be sure they record an address where you can be reached.

57. Search for impact fees through the county building department or Google your county name plus unspent or unexpended impact fees.

58. If you've been current with your utility payments (water, gas, electric) for at least a year ask to have them refunded.

    Now let's look at where your local and state government may find money.

59. Look for any state-specific programs in your state. For example, MediCal in California or Peach Care in Georgia.

60. Bringing it closer to home, keep the name search broad. You can usually limit it by city. Keep in mind that most cities started out as "Town of…", "Village of…" or "Municipality of…" so don't forget to try those searches.

    Look under the following names:

City of/Town of	Board of
Name of city	Dept. of
County of	County Commission
Name of county	County Court
State of	State Court
Name of state	Council of
School Board	Name of individual school

There may be others I haven't thought of. Let your imagination run wild!

THE GOVERNMENT

Search your Federal government. There are listings for every department of the federal government that I could think of. There may be some obscure office somewhere but the big ones are all present: Social Security, Medicare, Veterans Administration, and the one that blows me away, (and I can bring this up because I am squeaky clean on my taxes) the IRS. Who doesn't make darn sure that their check gets to Uncle Sam? It's not like they're hard to find!

The one I find the most humorous is the US Mint. I just find it funny that the people who make the money don't know they are missing money. And I'm pretty sure that if they are reading this, they are not finding the humor in it that I am.

IRS Refunds—Never got that tax refund? Go to **www.irs.ustreas.gov.** Click on "Where's My Refund?" on the right. You'll need your Social Security or Taxpayer ID number, the filing status and the exact whole dollar amount of your return. You can also call 1-800-829-1040, but you'll still need the information listed above.

You have three years to claim it. After that, the government keeps it.

Veteran's Administration —VA benefits are not benefits if you don't take advantage of them. Some of these do not involve getting money. They are simply free services that I feel are important to share. Here are some of the highlights:

- Vietnam Veterans diagnosed with a disease recognized as being related to exposure to Agent Orange may be eligible for service-connected compensation.

- VA's National Suicide Prevention Hotline is available 24/7 for those feeling alone, depressed or hopeless. 1-800-273-TALK (8255)

- Vets4Warriors is a peer-to-peer suicide prevention counseling service geared toward members and veterans of the National Guard. Help is available 24 hours a day by calling (855) VET-TALK (838-8255) or online at **www.vets4warriors.com**. It is staffed by veterans trained as counselors and is open to all branches of the military.

And there's a lot more. Go to **http://www1.va.gov/opa/myva/ index.asp**

A new program started in 2011 is Coaching into Care. It is a telephone service that provides assistance to family members and friends trying to encourage their Veteran to seek health care for possible readjustment and mental health issues. It's a national phone service that places priority on linking Veterans with benefits and services available in their own communities. If you think your Veteran friend or family member is having a difficult time and could benefit from readjustment counseling or mental health care, please utilize the Coaching into Care service: call 1-888-823-7458 or email **CoachingIntoCare@va.gov**.

Find information about survivor aid and benefits here:

http://www.vba.va.gov/survivors/agencies.htm

The VA holds returned life insurance payments, such as those for dividend checks, premium refunds or life insurance payout, indefinitely. Check the Veterans Affairs Web site at **https://insurance.va.gov/liability/ufsearch.htm**

A program administered through the Department of Justice is the Radiation Exposure Compensation Act (RECA). The RECA coverage is limited to the atmospheric nuclear testing program conducted by the U.S. after World War II. The Act only provides compensation for an individual who contracted a covered cancer resulting from their exposure. Further details are available at **http://www.justice.gov/civil/common/reca.html**

Military medals found in safe deposit boxes are excluded in some states like Illinois and Missouri from being sold at auction. The medals are displayed at events throughout the state in an attempt to reunite them with the rightful owner or heir,

Financial Management Service (*Based in part on public domain text from the Financial Management Services Web site*) There is no government-wide, centralized information service or database on how unclaimed government assets can be obtained. Each individual federal agency maintains its own records. The titles and addresses for all federal agencies are available in The United States Government Manual which is available in the reference section of most public libraries.

You must determine the type of benefit or payment that could be involved, the date on which the payment was expected, and how the payment should have been made. Given this information, the agency responsible for certifying any payment due should be able to assist you in determining the current status of any payment involved.

Professional finders file a Freedom of Information Act request to obtain the information on checks that are returned to the government. There is a check number provided, but no information about to whom the check was issued, or the amount. They then file another FOIA requesting the issuing information on the returned check number. This has the name of the person and the amount of the check. With that information, they search for the owner of the property.

http://www.fms.treas.gov/faq/unclaimed.html

USA.gov-- The headline reads. "The Government may owe you money."
http://www.usa.gov/Citizen/Topics/Money_Owed.shtml

COURTS

US Bankruptcy Court—Approximately $200 million dollars is waiting to be claimed. If you are a creditor of a person or corporation that has declared bankruptcy, you may have unclaimed monies due. Upon providing full proof of the right to funds held by the court, a claimant may obtain an order directing disbursement of unclaimed funds 28 U.S.C. 2042.

After five years, the money gets returned to the Treasury Department under the claimant's name, and can be claimed through them. There are also listings for Bankruptcy Court/US Bankruptcy Court on the unclaimed property sites.

On top of that, most businesses that have closed their doors due to financial failure also have listings on the missing money site. That is something you can bring to the court's attention if you are still owed money.

Check **http://www.uscourts.gov/court_locator.aspx** to find the bankruptcy court where the case was filed. The Wisconsin site will allow you to search by name. **http://www. wiwb.uscourts.gov/UnclaimedFunds/index.html**

Each state's forms vary slightly so it's best to ask that the proper form be sent to you. It's called Petition to Claim Unclaimed Funds from the US Treasury. You'll need to have it notarized. Notary services are usually available for free at your bank or your insurance agency.

You can stay on top of the court actions regarding your claim as a creditor by signing up for Electronic Bankruptcy Noticing, a free service that allows court notices to be transmitted electronically delivering them faster and more conveniently. Sign up for it here: **http://ebn.uscourts.gov/index.adp**

Class Actions—In general, 95 percent of class action lawsuit funds go unclaimed, according to Scott Hardy, president of Top Class Actions.

Have you ever received one of those postcards in the mail stating that you may be entitled to a proposed settlement from a class action lawsuit and then you never hear anything else? Search this site that is free to viewers. Submit your claims on open lawsuits at **http://www.TopClassActions.com**. Find out what lawsuits you might be entitled to participate in at http://www.Legafi.com.

Child Support Payments—If you owe child support payments and have listings on the state unclaimed property site, you may never get to see that money. Some states are enacting legislation to allow the unclaimed property funds to be intercepted when the owner is behind on child support. The Monroe County Daily in Maryland announced on Sept. 30, 2010 that the state treasurer, in the initial remittance of funds totaling $458,403 from the intercepted accounts, helped 1,281 families.

Another aspect of lost child support is called undeliverable or undistributable child support. When a check is received from the non-custodial parent and the account number is wrong or the name is illegible, the money received can't be credited to the correct account.

Google your state name plus undeliverable or undistributable or unclaimed child support. Be forewarned that there is a web site named unclaimedchildsupport.com that will charge you to search. Don't do it!

Remember to keep the child support folks informed of your change of address or name so you get your money. Putting in a change of address with the post office doesn't get the information to the child support office unless their envelope states Address Correction Requested. Even then, it can be missed. A change of address with the post office lasts for one year.

One more thing, you can enter Child Support in the Last Name; there are listings. Perhaps money you are owed has not made it to the child support office and is being held by the state. Encourage them to check.

Here are some direct links:

Florida—http://dor.myflorida.com/dor/childsupport/payment.html

Illinois—Cook County: Search by name or case year, division code and case number. www.cookcountyclerkofcourt.org/?section=CASEINFOPage&CASEINFOPage=4310

Illinois—Will County—For more information, call (815) 740-8017. Alphabetical list with the dollar amount. More than $79,000 in one county! www.willcountycircuitcourt.com/csdollars/CSDOLLARS.htm

Indiana—Elkhart County: Some of these listings include overpayments back to the birth year 1951; so I think some of them may be for the parent. www.elkhartcountyprosecutor.com/php/programs.services/child.support/unclaimed.child.support.php

Michigan—Enter the name as it would appear on your child support payments; and the last four digits of your Social Security number.
www.michigan.gov/som/0,1607,7-192-29929-107523--SERV,00.html
North Carolina—Unclaimed child support payments are listed on the state site. http://info.dhhs.state.nc.us/olm/manuals/dss/cse/man/CSEcP-20.htm#P2983_307476

Ohio—Franklin County Auditor: There are more than just child support payments here. You can also find lost heir accounts, vendor payments, proceeds from Sheriff's sales, Restitution payments and jury/witness fees. There is a disclaimer: "The Franklin County Auditor's Office does not hold funds from companies in Ohio." Search for those on the state site.
www.franklincountyauditor.com/fiscal/unclaimed-funds.cfm
Ohio—Summit County: Nine pages of listings! www.co.summit.oh.us/prosecutor/unclaimedmoney.htm

Oregon—Holds on to the funds for two years prior to turning it over to the state. You'll need the last four digits of your Social Security number, or your Oregon Child Support case number.
https://justice.oregon.gov/unclaimed/index.aspx

South Carolina—Access the SC Dept. of Social Services. Search alphabetically by last name at www.state.sc.us/dss/csed/abandprop.htm
Also check out the Spartanburg County Clerk of Court that has more than $900,000 in unclaimed child support and res-

titution.   **www.spartanburgcounty.org/govt/depts/coc/ UnclaimedFunds.htm**

Wisconsin—Alphabetical list. Go here: **http://dcf.wisconsin.gov/bcs/unclaimed_funds.htm**

Remember to Google your state name plus unclaimed, or undelivered, or undistributable child support. Avoid fee-based sites.

BANKING, FINANCIAL SERVICES, STOCKS

National Credit Union Administration—(*From public domain text on the ncua.gov Web site.*) When a credit union with federal insurance is liquidated, NCUA's Asset Management and Assistance Center (AMAC) is responsible for paying the share accounts to the members. Share accounts claimed within the 18-month insurance period are paid at their full insured amount. At the expiration of the 18-month insurance period, shares that are not claimed are considered uninsured and written down to share in the loss to the NCUSIF. Even if shares are uninsured when they are claimed, there may still be a distribution.

On rare occasions, the liquidation of a credit union may result in surplus funds. If a surplus remains, a distribution to the shareholders is required. This may occur several years after the credit union is liquidated and it is sometimes difficult to locate these members. Here is a PDF download of unclaimed deposits: **http://www.ncua.gov/resources/assetmgmtcenter/unclaimed.aspx**

Federal Deposit Insurance Corporation (FDIC)—When a participating bank fails, the FDIC acts as receiver until the new bank takes over, as Chase did in 2008 when Washington Mutual failed. The dormant accounts, in this case defined as those that have not had activity for three years or more, were sent to the state of the customer's last known address. This happened in April 2010. Monies in these accounts ceased earning interest on March 31, 2010. For information specifically about the WaMu failure, go to: **www.fdic.gov/bank/individual/ failure/wamu.html**

I don't know if this applies to all the FDIC monies that go to the states, but in Oregon, the unclaimed property site states "After ten years, the money must be returned to the FDIC." I couldn't find anything on the FDIC Web site that confirmed this. No one I spoke to at the FDIC was aware of this.

In the case of a bank being shut down completely by federal regulators, your insured deposits, up to the limit, should still available through the FDIC. The limit varies depending on when the bank was closed. Search by your name, business name, the bank name, city or state. For details, go to **http:// www2.fdic.gov/funds/index.asp**

Savings Bonds—There are an estimated 40 million unredeemed savings bonds for the American public worth approximately $16.5 billion dollars. Many of them have stopped earning interest. That's like having your money stuffed in a mattress.

A bill is currently in Congress that would allow the Treasury Department to turn the listings over to the state unclaimed property sites, making it easier for people to locate them. The House bill is HR 4198. In the senate, it is S827. This bill was referred to the Senate Committee on Finance in April, 2009. You can follow its progress, or lack of it, by going to **http:// thomas.loc.gov.**

(From public domain text on the US Treasury Web site.)

- Each year, 25,000 payments are returned to the Department of the Treasury as undeliverable.

- Billions of dollars in savings bonds have stopped earning interest but haven't been cashed.

- Treasury Hunt tells you about savings bonds that are no longer earning interest. If you have these savings bonds, cash or reinvest them so your money can start working for you again.

- The system only provides information on Series E bonds issued in 1974 and after.

- Most records for registered Treasury notes and bonds can be searched through this system.

- The site provides information on what to do for undeliverable bonds.

- Due to the Privacy Act of 1974, if you are not the owner or co-owner, the Treasury Department is limited in the information it can provide. If you are a legal heir, contact them anyway and see what you need to submit.

Check the issue date on your savings bonds and then visit: **www.treasurydirect.gov/indiv/research/securities/res_ securities_stoppedearninginterest.htm**
Or go to:

http://www.treasurydirect.gov/indiv/tools/tools_treasury-hunt.htm

Stocks—Transfer agents handle the administrative work of stocks. If you are contacted by a search firm and determine that it may be about stock that you own, you can usually find the name of the transfer agent by visiting the investor relations section of the company's website. Contact the transfer agent directly and see if you can intercept it.

Transfer agents must comply with SEC Rule 17Ad-17 of the Securities Exchange Act of 1934 which requires them to search for all lost shareholders. Two searches are required.

The first is done between 3 and 12 months of an account being identified as lost. The second search is done 6-12 months after the first search was completed.

Shareholders are a favorite market of professional finders. There is a lot of money to be made for the finders all in the name of "keeping the money from going to the state." If you wait for it to go to the state, you get your entire amount for free. If the transfer agent won't work with you, consider this:

Look at the above rule. Figure the account had to have had no activity for at least a year for the holder to go to the SEC. By the time both of those searches are done, the property has been sitting for 2-3 years.

Check the escheat rules for your state. Many states are trending toward decreased dormancy periods from five years down to three years.

If the finder's fee is 35 percent and you wait for it to go to the state where you get the full amount for free, you've earned a good guaranteed rate of return.

Read the tips at the end of the book to find out how to keep your stocks "active."

Investors Claims Funds—(*Based on public domain text on the SEC Web site*) are managed through the Securities and Exchange Commission. This page lists the SEC enforcement cases in which a Receiver, Disbursement Agent, or Claims Administrator has been appointed. Funds that are recovered and available for investors will be distributed according to an approved plan.

In addition to seeing whether a claims fund has been established, you may want to find out whether a private class action has been filed against the company you invested in. If you're aware of violations of the securities laws, please report it to the SEC by using the online complaint form.

If your broker-dealer has gone out of business, you can visit the website of the Securities Investor Protection Corporation (www.sipc.org) to find out whether your firm is the subject of a liquidation proceeding and how you can obtain a claim form. **www.sec.gov/divisions/enforce/claims.htm**

Housing and Urban Development/FHA refunds (*Based on public domain text on the HUD Web site*) HUD is not liable for a distributive share that remains unclaimed six years from the date the notification was first sent to the last known address of the mortgagor.

Also really important is that the rules governing eligibility for premium refunds and distributive share payments are based on the financial status of the FHA insurance fund and are subject to change.

You may be eligible for a refund of a portion of the insurance premium if you:

- Acquired your loan after Sept. 1, 1983

- Paid an up-front mortgage insurance premium at closing, and

- Did not default on your mortgage payment

Review your settlement papers or check with your mortgage company to determine if you paid an up-front premium.

You may be eligible for a share of any excessive earnings from the Mutual Mortgage Insurance Fund if you:

- Originated your loan before Sept. 1, 1983

- Paid on your loan for more than seven years, and

- Had your FHA mortgage insurance terminated before Nov. 5, 1990

There are some exceptions. Check the Web site for more information.
www.hud.gov/offices/hsg/comp/refunds/fhafact.cfm

FUN FACTS
Iowa has more than 2,000,000 shares of stock waiting to be claimed.

PERFORMANCE ROYALTIES

American Federation of Musicians (AFM) and American Federation of Television and Radio Artists (AFTRA) A list of individuals that have been credited for covered sound recordings is available at: **www.raroyalties.org/unclaimedchecks. html**

American Society of Composers, Authors and Musicians (ASCAP)
ASCAP members can log into their account via 'Member Access' to see if a royalty distribution check was issued, as well as make sure that their information is current. **www.ascap. com**

Broadcast Music, Inc. (BMI) According to the Web site, BMI turns the undeliverable royalty payments over to the state. Emails asking about the pre-escheat phase were ignored. **www. bmi.com/news/entry/233973**

Screen Actors Guild SAG has a site where you can search and see if you, as a performer, loan out, or as a beneficiary/heir of a performer have unclaimed residuals. Search at **www.sag.org/ content/search-unclaimed-residuals.**

SESAC Another Performing Rights Organization like BMI and ASCAP. **http://www.sesac.com/Repertory/ FindAffiliateList.aspx**

Sound Exchange is a non-profit performance rights organization that collects statutory royalties from satellite radio (such as SIRIUS XM), internet radio, cable TV music channels and similar platforms for streaming sound recordings. The Copyright Royalty Board, which is appointed by The U.S. Library of Congress, has entrusted SoundExchange as the sole entity in the United States to collect and distribute these digital performance royalties on behalf of featured recording artists, master rights owners (like record labels), and independent artists who record and own their masters. If you haven't registered with them, you may not be aware of the royalties they are holding for you. Contact them directly: **http://soundexchange. com.** Sound Exchange paid out a total of $810 million as of December 22, 2011.

Major recording companies may also have royalty listings. Check with the company that the artist was signed with. If the information is not available online, call and inquire.

RETIREMENT BENEFITS

Terminated 401K Plans— If the company you worked for terminated the 401K plan and they were unable to find you, keep reading.

A Qualified Termination Administrator is responsible for the termination. The US Department of Labor provides the guidelines they must follow. The QTA must follow defined search methods ending with using Social Security Administration or Internal Revenue Service letter-forwarding service as a last resort. If the search produces no results, the QTA can either rollover the money into a traditional IRA or transfer the money into a federally insured savings account.

The problem with the latter is that it comes with tax consequences that you aren't even aware that you incurred. You will have to pay ordinary income taxes plus the 10 percent penalty if you are not of retirement age.

In either case, if these eventually go to the state unclaimed property office, you may not recognize them as yours since you did not open the savings account or the IRA.

You can search for information about terminated plans by going to The Department of Labor Employee Benefits Security Administration:
http://askebsa.dol.gov/AbandonedPlanSearch/

National Registry of Unclaimed Retirement Benefits The National Registry is a nationwide, secure database listing of retirement plan account balances that have been left unclaimed.

This differs from the above listing in that these are active plans with inactive participants. Former employees can perform a free secure search to determine if they are entitled to any unpaid retirement account money. Employers can register (for free) the names of former employees who have left money with them. Search by the Social Security Number. **www.unclaimedretirementbenefits.com**

Pension Benefit Guaranty Corporation is holding $197 million in unclaimed private sector pensions for about 36,000 people. If you participated in a "defined benefit" pension plan (*not* a 401K, 403B or profit sharing plan) in a privately owned company that terminated, then transferred, the plan to PBGC, you may have money. "Defined benefit" pension plans are traditional pension plans which promise to pay a specific monthly amount to participants when they retire. You say you don't know if the pension was transferred to PBGC? It doesn't hurt to look! Search by the last name of the participant, the name of the company, or the state in which the company was located. Like all of the sites I have listed, this one is free to look up and free to claim. It is not a list of all people due pensions from PBGC. It is a list only of those people whom PBGC has not yet been able to contact directly. **http://search.pbgc.gov/mp/mp.aspx**

US Railroad Retirement Board Survivors of retired railroad employees that died between 1964 and 2001 may be entitled to receive a $2,000 life insurance benefit. Claimants can call MetLife at 1-800-310-7770 to determine eligibility. MetLife is solely responsible for determining if a claimant meets eligibility requirements. For online benefit information go to
   www.rrb.gov/mep/ben_services.asp

NY State Deferred Compensation Plan This is a list of participant uncashed checks that have been outstanding for four months or longer. If you have two or more checks outstanding, issuance of further checks may be suspended. If you find you name on the list, call 1-800-422-8463 for verification.

SC Retirement System Unclaimed Funds— If you ever worked for an employer covered by the Retirement Systems in South Carolina or left the covered employment more than one year ago and left your money in your retirement account, then search this site for inactive accounts: **https://www.retirement.sc.gov/inactive/entry.htm**

Other State Retirement Programs Each state has its own site for state retirement benefits. Google the name of your state and search for its retirement benefits.

FUN FACTS
States hold auctions of intangible property such as the contents of safe deposit boxes. Some are live auctions; some are on eBay. The money is held for the owners.

LIFE INSURANCE

Life Insurance Searches—It is estimated that more than $1 billion dollars goes unclaimed every year due to lost or unknown policies. I found the money from my father's estate as stock in an insurance company. I had a question and contacted them. At that point I found there was a life insurance policy that listed my half-sister as the beneficiary. It was only by that chance call that the policy came to light and she was able to file and get her money.

If you don't know if a loved one had one or more life insurance policies, here are six steps you can take.

1. Start with the agency they have their car or homeowner's insurance policy through. Look for insurance cards from insurance agents or any paperwork or policies. If you find a policy but can't find the insurance company that is listed, *Best's Insurance Reports* is available in the reference section in most libraries. It contains information about mergers and name changes in the insurance industry.

2. Check their cancelled checks for any premium payments to an insurance company. Don't forget to check the bank statement for any payments that were made electronically either to or from the insurance company.

3. When you're closing out the deceased's banking matters, ask their bank if they had a safe deposit box. If you don't have a key, you'll be charged to have them drill out the lock.

4. Check with former employers for any group life insurance policy your loved one may have participated in. If he or she was a union member, check with the union. Also check groups such as AARP or professional organizations they belonged to.

5. Review past IRS returns looking for a 1099-INT form with interest from an insurance company reported.

6. An often overlooked source is credit cards or the auto insurance policy that may carry an accidental death benefit. If your loved one died from an injury or accident, look into this.

The last recourse is go company by company. The state insurance office has a list of companies that operate in that state. Remember to search in each state where your loved one lived and may have purchased a policy.

I contacted several of the major insurers and got no response about their procedure for dormant accounts. There were very tight lipped. No one would clarify if the policies that go to the state are listed under the beneficiary's name or the policyholder's name or if it is listed on the state of the policyholder's last known address or the last known address of the beneficiary. I got no comment from any of them.

So I kept digging.

Here's what I found: Life insurance companies are not required to search for heirs or comb the obituaries to see if their policy holder died.

The dormancy period for a life insurance policy when there is no death reported in most cases is three years after what would have been the policy holder's 100th birthday. If your loved one died at age 70 and no one notified the life insurance company, you would have to wait 33 years before it appeared on the unclaimed property site. In the meantime, the life insurer is earning interest on the money or letting fees deplete it.

If a death has not been reported, and the dormant policy is turned over to the state, it goes to the state of the last know known address of the policyholder and is listed in the policy-holder's name. It does not become the property of the benefici-ary until the death is documented.

Some of the older whole life policies begin losing value after the policy holder reaches age 95. Read the fine print in the policy or check with your insurance agent.

What has come to light is that many of the companies use the Social Security Death Index to determine when they no longer need to make annuity payments to a policyholder. However they are not using the same resource to determine when they need to pay out on a life insurance benefit. Thirty-six states are looking into these practices. Where are the rest of them?

The American Council of Life Insurers (ACLI) has tips for how to determine if your loved one might have had a life insurance policy. Go to: **ww.acli.com/ACLI/consumers/ Life+Insurance/Locating+a+Missing+Policy/default.htm**

New York Life You can search NY Life's records of unclaimed assets remitted to the states for funds that may be owed to you or a member of your family. Under the "Search" option on the left, enter Unclaimed Funds Finder. If you find your loved one's name in the database, you can contact the state listed to claim these funds. **www.newyorklife.com/nyl/v/index.jsp?conten tId=9041&vgnextoid=244ca2b3019d2210a2b3019d22102 4301cacRCRD**

These are only the policies that have met the escheat criteria and were turned over to the state. If the policy is in the pre-escheat phase, it would still be held by the company. Contact them directly if you think your loved one had a policy through them.

Veterans Life Insurance The VA holds returned life insurance payments--such as those for dividend checks, premium refunds or life insurance payouts—indefinitely. Check the Veterans Affairs Web site at **https://insurance.va.gov/liability/ufsearch.htm**

Ohio Department of Insurance sets the standard by which other states should be measured when it comes to helping folks determine if their loved one who lived in Ohio had a life insurance policy that was purchased in that state.

On the home page, **http://www.insurance.ohio.gov**, click on Consumers on the left. From the drop-down menu select Find A Missing Life Insurance Policy. The service also provides information about annuity contracts purchased in Ohio. Print the request form. Fill out the form and have it notarized. Send it in with a copy of the certified death certificate.

If you don't have Internet access call (800) 686-1526 to request that a claim form be mailed to you. To request the form by mail, write to :

Missing Life Insurance/Annuity Search Request Service
Ohio Department of Insurance
Consumer Affairs-Life Unit
50 West Town St., Suite 300
Columbus, OH 43215

The department forwards your request along with the supporting documentation to all Ohio-licensed life insurance companies within 25 business days of receiving your request. You must be a beneficiary or executor of the estate to request this information.

Louisiana Department of Insurance site has useful tips for determining if someone had a life insurance policy and the company that issued it. They are a close second to Ohio in their helpfulness with helping people determine if their loved one bought life insurance in the state. You can search for policies that were issued in Louisiana and then contact the insurance company for further information. The site cannot be used to search for policies that were not purchased in Louisiana. You will need the deceased's social security number and date of death when you call. Go to: **www.ldi.la.gov/Licensing/Life_ Annuities/Life_Annuity_before_submit_request.htm**
    If that's too daunting a task, there are a couple of companies listed below that will perform the search for you for a fee.

Medical Information Bureau searches life insurance companies that are members of their organization. If your loved one had a policy with a company that is not a member of MIB, the search will not show the policy. The fee is $75. When they return their findings to you, you will also get the *Policy Locator Research Primer* that will provide additional sources for you to check. Go here: **www.mibsolutions.com**

The Lost Life Insurance Finder Expert charges more ($98.50) but searches 460 companies. The extent of their involvement is to help you with the submission, submit the query and answer any questions you may have. The companies reply directly to you. Go here: **www.l-lifeinsurance.com**

FindYourPolicy.com Michael Hartmann, a licensed life insurance agent, created this site after his father's passing. People can register the name of the company that they have a life insurance policy with so loved ones can find the information in a central location and know who to contact. It's free to register your information but searches are $9.95. It's a small price that probably keeps finders away. **www.FindYourPolicy.com**

INTERNATIONAL

The United States isn't the only country with unclaimed money.

Canada:
**http://ucbswww.bank-banque-canada.ca/Scripts/search_
english.cfm** Federally regulated bank or trust companies turn
the money over to the Bank of Canada when the account is
deemed dormant. Bank of Canada holds balances of $1,000 or
more for 100 years. Balances of less than $1,000 are held for 40
years. As of Dec, 2010 there were 1.3 million accounts worth
$433 million, the oldest dating back to 1900.

 Alberta: www.finance.alberta.ca/business/unclaimed_
property/index.html

 British Columbia: www.unclaimedpropertybc.ca They
have listings dating back to the late 1800s. On the Web site,
click Search for Unclaimed Property and then "Other Places to
Look" for an extensive list of additional sites in Canada.

 Quebec: www.revenu.gouv.qc.ca/en/bnr/default.aspx

The United Kingdom: www.unclaimedassets.co.uk/
 Also try: www.mylostaccount.org.uk/

 Bona Vacantia administers the estates of those who died
intestate without known kin and collects the assets of dissolved
companies and failed trusts. Check the list here: **http://www.
bonavacantia.gov.uk/output/**

 Citizen's Advice Bureau in Scotland will do a benefit
check for you to see if you may be entitled to benefits or tax

credits that you are not aware of. CAB advisers regularly find cases of people missing out on some sort of benefit or grant just because they weren't aware of it.

Ireland: Click Dormant Accounts on the left. www.ntma.ie

France: (Only available in French) www.afb.fr/Web/internet/interMain.nsf?OpenDatabase

Switzerland: www.swissbanking.org

Australia: www.fido.asic.gov.au/fido/fido.nsf/byheadline/Unclaimed+money+-+overview?openDocument

New Zealand: www.ird.govt.nz/unclaimed-money

Malaysia: Contact the Registrar of Unclaimed Moneys www.anm.gov.my

India: Dormant accounts and real estate are not turned over to a government agency but you can get help through www.fundtracers.com for a fee.

Kenya: Is establishing an unclaimed property office but was not done at press time.

COMPENSATION FUNDS

Holocaust Survivors—For information about Holocaust victims' unclaimed bank accounts and insurance funds, please call the Holocaust Claims Processing Office in the New York State Banking Department at (800) 695-3318, or online at www.claims.state.ny.us/. All deadlines to file claims relating to the Swiss Banks Settlement have expired. All claims and appeals through the International Commission on Holocaust Era Insurance Claims have also expired as of December 2006. The site, www.icheic.org, is maintained as a historical record. Also check out the following: Project HEART www.heart-website.org

The Claims Conference on Jewish Material Claims Against Germany is another site. Go to: www.claimscon.org

The Simon Wiesenthal Center: Provides claims procedures for locating Swiss, Swedish, French and British bank and insurance accounts.
www.wiesenthal.com/site/pp.asp?c=lsKWLbPJLnF&b=4441251

Radiation Exposure Compensation Act (RECA) is program administered through the Department of Justice. The Act's coverage is limited to the atmospheric nuclear testing program conducted by the US after World War II. The Act only provides compensation for an individual who has contracted a covered cancer following their exposure. Further details are available at http://www.justice.gov/civil/common/reca.html

Vaccine Injury Compensation Program—Individuals who believe they have been injured by a covered vaccine can file a claim against the Secretary of the Department of Health and Human Services in the US Court of federal claims seeking compensation from the trust fund. Eligible claimants can recover compensation for vaccine injury-related medical and rehabilitative expenses, pain and suffering, and lost wages. Details can be found at **http://www.justice.gov/civil/common/vicp.html**

9/11 Victim Compensation Fund provides compensation to any individual (or personal representative of a deceased individual) who suffered physical harm or was killed as a result of the terrorist-related airplane crashes on Sept. 11, 2001, or the debris removal that took place in the immediate aftermath. Go here: **http://www.vcf.gov**

Victims of violent crime—Most states have a Crime Victim Compensation Program to help with medical bills, loss of earnings and even funeral expenses. This applies to children too. Check with your local victim advocate for more information. You can also Google the name of your state followed by Crime Victim Compensation.

MISCELLANEOUS MONEY

The United States Free Public Directory has some listings by county for unclaimed property that is in the pre-escheat phase. To search, enter your state under Search Public Records by State near the top. Then in the same place, there will be a drop down menu that says Search Public Records by Category. Scroll down to unclaimed property. Go down on the page. The first listing will be the unclaimed property link for the state. Counties that have information will be listed below that. There are also loads of other useful links available on this site. http://publicrecords.onlinesearches.com/UnitedStates. htm

Unpaid Foreign Claims—The Foreign Claims Awards are certified to the Department of the Treasury for payment by the Foreign Claims Settlement Commission (FCSC), an independent quasi-judicial federal agency, which is administratively a component of the U.S. Department of Justice. The FCSC determines the validity and valuation of claims of U.S. nationals for loss of property in foreign countries, as authorized by Congress or following government-to-government settlement agreements. These losses can occur as either a result of nationalization of property by foreign governments or from damage to or loss of property as a result of military operations, or injury to both civilian and military personnel.

The Department of the Treasury's role is to ensure that the FCSC claimants receive the proper payment amount as authorized in the public law that governs each Foreign Claims Program. **www.fms.treas.gov/tfc/index.html**

There are listings by name for Germany, Vietnam, and War Claims.

Germany: **www.fms.treas.gov/tfc/germany-claims.html**
Vietnam: **www.fms.treas.gov/tfc/vietnam-claims.html**
War Claims: **www.fms.treas.gov/tfc/war-claims.html**

Native American Indians (*Taken in part from public domain text from the Individual Indian Money Account Information brochure.*) The Office of the Special Trustee (OST) for American Indians is seeking current addresses for Individual Indian Money (IIM) account holders. IIM accounts are established for individual trust beneficiaries. These accounts can be created for a number of reasons. Some examples include:

- You are the original allottee of a parcel of land.

- You are an heir to the original allottee of a parcel of Indian trust land and have inherited the land through probate.

- You received a trust asset through a gift deed.

- You received a per capita trust payment from the tribe, a tribal settlement or a judgment award.

As of Dec. 5, 2007, there was over $70 million in trust for more than 70,000 people whose whereabouts were unknown. There is a link to a press release about not using "finders" to get the money. If you have questions, call 1-888-678-6836 from

7 a.m.—6 p.m. (Mountain Time Zone) Monday-Friday; and 8 a.m.—noon on Saturday. **http://www.doi.gov/ost/**

Oil and Mineral Royalties—If you are contacted about oil or mineral royalties for a deceased relative, chances are there was an accountant involved for the purposes of filing income taxes. Look for old IRS forms and check if there is a preparer's name at the bottom of the 1040. Contact that person. You may need to provide documentation that shows you are the administrator of the estate.

John R. Thomason, an attorney in Houston Texas who is board certified in oil, gas and mineral law, said the first step is to determine who in your family may have owned it and where the property is. If you can find out what county the property is in, (everything revolves around this) check the real property records. Run indexes, check the grantee records to see if mineral or royalty rights were received and grantor records to see if they were passed on. It may be worthwhile to hire a professional Landman who is well-versed in the area (**www.landman.org** is the professional organization) or an abstractor from a title company.

"You may need to go back several generations or at least for the lifetime of the ancestor," said Thomason. Also check the ad valorem property tax records.

If a company wants to drill on a property but has been unsuccessful in their attempt to locate the mineral rights owner, the company can petition the court. If the judge is satisfied with their attempts to locate the owners, a receiver is appointed. So another avenue is to check with the clerk of the court to see if there has been any receivership actions filed. Any monies that are generated from the drilling project are held for the owners to claim.

Roger Soape, a Certified Professional Landman in Houston Texas, said "There can be a lot of research required to develop adequate ownership information to get companies to release funds to royalty owners. Usually, though, proceeds which are unclaimed or owed to unknown persons are turned over to the state where the property is located."

Old Stock Certificates/Mining Certificates—The Securities and Exchange Commission has a site (**www.sec.gov/answers/oldcer.htm**) that refers you to people who, for a fee, can help you evaluate the worth of your old certificates.

Even if the company is no longer in business, they may have value if that company was taken over by another. They may also have value as a collectible item. Check at **www.scripophily.com** for collectible value.

Postal Money Orders—Lost damaged or stolen money orders can be traced here: **www.usps.com/missingmoneyorders**

Lost Luggage—This topic and the one that follows were reader suggestions. Lost luggage goes to the Unclaimed Baggage Center in Scottsdale, Alabama. It's the largest tourist attraction in Alabama bringing 800,000 people through its doors every year. Also included are unclaimed items from bus lines, air freight and the lost and found department of airports.

The bags are opened. The items are sorted, cleaned and put up for sale. This is the part you're not going to want to hear.

You can't just go there and lay claim to your stuff. By the time it reaches the UBC, the airline has paid you for your loss. The unidentified baggage and its contents are now the property of the airline. And they ship it off to Alabama.

Here's my thought...you know that camera in your phone? Use it to take a picture of your luggage before you leave. It would be easier for the airline crew to *see* a picture of the missing item since they have to *look* for it. Plus, if it gets damaged, you can show that it wasn't damaged when you checked it in.

Another helpful hint is that when you're headed to your destination, put the hotel or destination address on the luggage tag with your name and the dates you are staying there. Of course you should also have your name and permanent address on the inside as well. Luggage manufacturers should include a spot inside the luggage for this purpose.

Recovered stolen property—Propertyroom.com is an auction site for police and other municipal agencies that need to auction items. Some of these items can be recovered stolen property for which the rightful owner could not be found. There are also individual sellers, but they are carefully screened. Only 5-10 per year are added.

TIPS TO PREVENT YOUR MONEY FROM GOING TO THE STATE

- When you move, know that the change of address card you fill out with the post office is only valid for one year. As mail gets forwarded to you, change the address with each company. Even if the company has Address Correction Requested on the envelope, don't assume your information is going to be updated. Don't forget to change your physical address with companies that you get ebills from or do online banking with. There's a checklist at the end of this section to help make sure you don't miss anyone.

- Utility deposits are a common source of unclaimed property. If you've paid your electric, water or gas bill on time for a year or more, ask if the utility company will credit your deposit back to your account. Crediting your account can have an advantage over getting a check because you have the value instantly, and there is no chance for a lost check.

  If they say it happens automatically, ask when you can expect it and look for it. If you don't get it, follow up with them. If you don't get the refund while you are living in the residence, make sure the utility companies have your correct new address.

- Cash every check as soon as possible.

- Always make sure you get your final paycheck from an employer. As an example, if your last day of work is the first day of the new pay period, you will have two checks, not one. There will be one check from the pay period that just ended, plus another check from the following pay cycle from the one day from the new pay period.

- Notify the 401K or 403B administrator and the employer sponsored insurance plans (life, health, dental) of your new address when you move. Just because you give your employer the information doesn't mean it will be shared with the others. Also, if you change jobs notify the retirement plan of this change also so your money can follow you.

- Have some activity on your financial accounts at least once a year. Many people mistakenly believe that if their savings account is earning interest that it counts as activity. It doesn't! Activity is defined as customer initiated activity. Put $5 in. Take $5 out. Call to check on the balance even if you already know it. Do *something*. Make it a birthday present to yourself every year. Also know that just because you have activity on one account doesn't mean it counts toward your other accounts (savings/checking/CDs/Investments/retirement, etc.) even within the same institution.

- When it comes to stocks, customer initiated activity does *not* include sending back your proxy vote according to a representative from New York Bank of Mellon Shareholder Services. At least once a year, call to check on the account balance, request a statement or verify your address. Don't rely on anyone else to do this for you. Considering that the largest amount paid out in the United States to an individual was $6.1 million dollars for a stock claim, there can be a lot of money at stake. If it gets to the point that you are getting letters saying the transfer agent hasn't heard from you and your holdings might get turned over to the state unless they hear from you, then reply immediately!

- Notify everyone listed above and anyone else you do business with when you have a name change.

- Make a list of your assets. Make sure someone knows where your important financial documents are in case of your death.

- If you have a life insurance policy and your beneficiary moves, notify the insurance company of the new address.

- When closing out your loved one's finances at the bank, ask them to check if there was a safe deposit box.

- If your mortgage lender foreclosed on your home, notify them of an address where you can be reached in case the home sold for more than you owed. You are entitled to the amount paid in excess of your balance. The same holds true for tax liens/deeds sold. Make sure the property tax office has an address for you.

- Your digital assets may never be found until they are turned over to the state. Your online accounts, such as PayPal, iTunes or PartyPoker may have credits. Perhaps you have an eBay or Amazon store. Do you have an online-only bank account or other investments that never generate postal mail? Make sure your heirs have access to your login name and password so the account balances don't get escheated.

  In addition, there is a wealth of online value to your digital possessions such as domain names, your irreplaceable digital photos and more. (Sometimes this is about more than just money.)

  There are two services that allow you to catalog all these digital treasures so your designated person has access to them after your passing.

  Entrustet.com's free offering is easy to use and allows a generous listing of information. The premium program is $30/year and has no lifetime membership available.

  Legacylocker.com allows only three listings for free and one beneficiary. You can upgrade for an annual fee of $29.99 or a lifetime registration of $299.99. These amounts are found under the FAQ #18.

CHANGE OF NAME/ADDRESS
CHECKLIST

You can use this list as a reminder of places to notify when you have a change of name and address to prevent your money from getting turned over to the state because the company lost track of you. Not all of these involve money. Not all of them will apply to everyone. The list is meant to be comprehensive on many levels. You can also use it as a reminder of assets to be listed or places to notify upon the death of a loved one.

Banking:
Checking
Savings
Mortgage
CD
Safe Deposit Box
Retirement
Other

Retirement/Investments:
401K
403B
SEP
IRA
Roth
Pension

Mutual Funds
Stocks
Bonds
Savings Bonds
Annuities
Trust
Other

Insurance:
Medical/Supplemental
Mail order prescriptions/medical supplies
Dental
Vision
FSA
HSA
Medicare
Whole Life
Term Life

Professional:
Doctors
Dentist
Orthodontist
Optometrist
Mental Health
Therapy
Attorney
CPA
Hospital
Lab

Radiology
ER

Utilities:
Electric
Water
Gas
Telephone
Cell
Internet
Satellite radio
Trash pick-up

Governmental:
Social Security Administration
Internal Revenue Service
Veteran's Administration
Vehicle Registration
Local tax collector
State Treasurer (states with income taxes)

Licenses:
Driver's License/DMV
CDL
Vehicle
Boat
Airplane
Personal Watercraft
Professional (MD, RN, Cosmetology, etc)
Home-based Business

Hunting
Fishing
Pet/Pet ID tag on collar

Subscriptions:
Newspapers
Magazines
Newsletters
(Blank) of the month club

Credit Cards:
Visa
Master Card
American Express
Discover
Retail Stores
Gas

Accounts Receivable:
Employer
Child Support
Alimony
Commissions
Consulting Fees
Performance Royalties
Oil and Mineral Royalties
Timber Royalties
Bankruptcy
Lawsuit
Jury Duty pay

Retail:
>   Layaway
>   Savings Clubs (Sam's, Costco, etc)

Cultural:
>   Church
>   Library
>   School
>   College
>   Alumni Association
>   Sorority/Fraternity
>   Museums
>   Theatre
>   Botanical
>   Civic Organizations

Miscellaneous:
>   Pet Microchip
>   Pre-paid tolls

BEST PRACTICES

When a state offers something really unique to help people get their missing money, they deserve recognition. These are some of my favorites in alphabetical order by state.

California—Kudos to State Comptroller John Chiang for bringing to light the practice of life insurers. An audit showed that most life insurers would use the Social Security Death Index to determine when an annuitant died and the company could stop paying the annuity. However, they did not use the same database to determine when a policy holder died and a death benefit was due. This is not illegal. Thirty-six additional states have looked into this practice. Where are the others?

California—The Golden State offers something other states don't. Listings from holders are posted on the unclaimed property site for six months before they get turned over to the state. What this means for consumers is they have an opportunity to claim their money directly from the holder which is significantly easier than going through the state.

Iowa makes detailed information about finders easily accessible under their FAQs. Why doesn't every state provide this important information on their Web site? It's the right thing to do for their citizens.

Louisiana—This is actually a tip of the hat to the State Department of Insurance. The Louisiana Department of Insurance maintains a database containing electronic contact information for all life insurance companies which have policies in force in Louisiana. They have a process in place if you are trying to find out if your loved one who lived in Louisiana had a life insurance policy. This makes it much easier and there is no fee for this valuable consumer service. It only works if the person bought insurance while living in Louisiana.

Maryland—This is one of the states that will intercept listings from the state unclaimed property site for the non-custodial parent when that person is behind on child support.

Missouri—This state has begun putting kiosks in the county tax offices. So when you go to pay your property taxes or auto tag, you can take a moment and check if you have money to pay for that! Granted, some folks just mail in the payment and miss this opportunity. But I think it's a great way to reach out and make the search process easy for state residents.

North Dakota—I love this! I wish my state did it. In addition to searching by name, North Dakota will let you search by city. I would love to be able to find money for neighbors that I may not otherwise think of.

Ohio—Kudos to the Ohio Department of Insurance. Submit the form to them if your loved one might have had a life insurance policy or annuity that was purchased in Ohio. The info is sent out to the Ohio insurance companies. If they have information about a policy they are required to respond within 21 days if you are an authorized person.

Texas offers two great services. If you are a major corporation with lots of listings, contact the unclaimed property office and they will assist you so you don't have to file dozens—or hundreds—of individual claims. Also, you can choose to donate your listing to a charity.

Wisconsin's State Treasurer Kurt Schuller has a blog where once a week he will select a county and post the names of the people or businesses with the top five listings based on dollar amount (which is not shown). He doesn't wait for people to happen across the listing. He shines a spotlight on it in the hopes that someone reading it will know the people or the business listed and will tell them.

He also went out to nursing homes to assist elderly residents in searching for their missing money.

STATE UNCLAIMED PROPERTY CONTACT INFO

I listen to reader feedback. One of the requests was to have the state contact information available for those who don't have computer access.

Here it is.

I've included two additional items. One is how often the state site updates its information. The other is state-specific information about professional finders.

Let me tell you…as proficient as I am at searching online, finding this information about finders was a real challenge. If I had to read through the state statutes, I included the number of the statute. If you want to search yourself, here's a hint based on my experience: start at the bottom and work up. For example, New Jersey's unclaimed property law is 245 pages. The information about finders is on page 240.

I don't understand why states don't provide this information front and center on their site. In some cases, there was nothing whatsoever online. I feel states owe their residents this level of information.

There were some things in common among many states that adopted the Uniform Unclaimed Property Act. Check with your own state to see if these apply:

- You can claim a fee is unconscionable.

- Some states have limitations on the fee, but if you are willing, they can be exceeded with a full disclosure form that specifies the nature of the property, who it is from, the dollar amount, and the amount you will receive after the finder's fee.

- In the case of oil or mineral royalties that are due to you, the finder cannot take a portion of your holdings, only the dollar amount that is due you.

Remember that these rules only apply to listings on the state unclaimed property sites. If you get contacted about money that is in the pre-escheat phase or money that will not get turned over to the state, you're on your own. But knowing what your state standard is may give you some bargaining room. Unfortunately, Delaware and West Virginia have no laws in place on this topic.

Alabama
Office of the State Treasurer
Unclaimed Property Division
P.O. Box 302520
Montgomery, AL 36130-2520
(334) 242-9614
(888) 844-8400
Updated: Every several months
Finders: Contract is void if it was entered into from the date the property was presumed abandoned until 24 months after it has been in the possession of the state treasurer. 35-12-93

Alaska
State of Alaska
Treasury Division
P.O. Box 110405
Juneau, AK 99811-0405
(907) 465-3726
Updated: As reports come in
Finders: Fees limited to 10% on property above $500; 20% on property less than $500. No requirements or licenses.

Arizona
Department of Revenue
Unclaimed Property Unit
P.O. Box 29026
Phoenix, AZ 85038-9026
(602) 364-0380
(877) 492-9957
Updated: Every 14 days

Finders: Fee cannot exceed 30%. Must be currently licensed private investigators. Money must have been in state possession for 2 years.

Arkansas
Auditor of State
Unclaimed Property Division
1401 W Capitol Ave, Suite 325
Little Rock, AR 72201-1811
(501) 682-6000
(800) 252-4648
Updated: Annually in the spring. Changing to a new system that will allow more frequent updates.
Finders: Maximum fee is 10%.

California
Office of State Controller
Unclaimed Property Division
P.O. Box 942850
Sacramento, CA 94250-5873
(916) 323-2827
(800) 992-4647
Updated: Monthly
Finders: Fee not more than 10% except for County Probated Estates which have no limit.

Colorado
Department of the Treasury
Great Colorado Payback
1580 Logan, Suite 500
Denver, CO 80203

(303) 866-6070
(800) 825-2111
Updated: As reports come in
Finders: Fee is limited to 20%. Property must be in possession
of the state for at least 24 months.

Connecticut
Office of the State Treasurer
Unclaimed Property Division
55 Elm St.
Hartford, CT 06106
(860) 702-3125
(800) 833-7318
Updated: As reports come in.
Finders: Fee is limited to 10%

Delaware
Delaware Bureau of Unclaimed Property
P.O. Box 8931
Wilmington, DE 19899
(302) 577-8220
Updated: annually, end of October.
Finders: No rules

District of Columbia
Office of Finance and Treasury
Unclaimed Property Unit
1101 4th St SW, Suite W800-B
Washington DC 20024
(202) 442-8181
Updated: Weekly

Finders: Fee limited to 10%. May exceed this if the agreement is in writing, signed by owner, specifies nature and value of property and the holder. Owner may assert at any time that the fee is excessive or unjust. Must be in possession at least 7 months. § 41-137.

Florida
Department of Financial Services
Unclaimed Property Bureau
P.O. Box 8599
Tallahassee, FL 32314-8599
(850) 413-5555
(888) 258-2253
Updated: Monthly
Finders: Fees are limited to 20% up to a max of $1,000 per account. This may be exceeded if the original contract you signed contains a full disclosure. Call for details. Must be licensed as a CPA, attorney or private investigator.

Georgia
Georgia Department of Revenue
Unclaimed Property
4245 International Pkwy, Suite A
Hapeville, GA 30354-3918
(404) 968-0490
Updated: Daily
Finders: Fee is not to exceed 10%. Listing must be in state possession for at least 24 months. §44-12-224

Hawaii
Department of Budget and Finance

Unclaimed Property Program
P.O. Box 150
Honolulu, HI 96810
(808) 586-1589
Updated: Monthly
Finders: No limit on fees, but owner can claim it is "unconscionable." Listing must be in state possession for at least 24 months. §523A-25

Idaho
State Treasurer's Office
Unclaimed Property Program
P.O. Box 83720
Boise, ID 83720-9101
(208) 332-2942
(877) 388-2942
10 year limit to claim
Updated: Annually in January
Finders: No regulations on finders or limit on fees. Listing must be in state possession at least 24 months.

Illinois
Office of the State Treasurer
Unclaimed Property Division
P.O. Box 19495
Springfield, IL 62794-9495
(217) 785-6998
(866) 458-7327
Listings prior to 1992 and those less than $5 are not on web site. Call to check.
Updated: Weekly

Finders: Fees are limited to 10%. Must be registered as detectives with the IL Dept. of Professional Regulation. Listing must be in state possession at least 24 months.

Indiana
Office of the Attorney General
Unclaimed Property Division
P.O. Box 2504
Greenwood, IN 46142
(866) 462-5246
25 year limit to claim
Updated: Daily
Finders: May charge up to 10%.

Iowa
Great Iowa Treasure Hunt
Lucas State Office Building
321 E 12th St, 1st Floor
Des Moines, IA 50319
(515) 281-5367
Updated: As reports come in
Finders: Fees are limited to 15%. Must be licensed as private investigators. Listing must be in state possession at least 24 months.

Kansas
Kansas State Treasurer
Unclaimed Property Division
900 SW Jackson, Suite 100
Topeka, KS 66612-1235

(785) 296-4165
(800) 432-0386
Updated: Annually and as reports come in
Finders: Fee is not to exceed 15%. Listing must be in state possession at least 24 months.

Kentucky
Kansas State Treasurer
Unclaimed Property Division
1050 US Hwy 127 South, Suite 100
Frankfort, KY 40601
(502) 564-4722
(800) 465-4722
Updated: Nightly
Finders: Fees limited to 10%. Agreements made between the date the property was assumed abandoned and extending through 24 months after the property was delivered to the State Treasurer are void and unenforceable. 393.117

Louisiana
Office of the State Treasurer
Unclaimed Property Division
P.O. Box 91010
Baton Rouge, LA 70821-9010
(225) 219-9400
(888) 925-4127
Updated: Almost every night
Finders: Fee limited to 10%. Listing must be in state possession for at least 24 months.

Maine

Office of the State Treasurer
Attn: Unclaimed Property
39 State House Station
Burton M. Cross Bldg. 3rd Floor
111 Sewall St,
Augusta, ME 04333-0039
(207) 624-7470
(888) 283-2808
Updated: Nightly
Finders: Agreements made more than 24 months and less than 36 months after the listing is presumed abandoned are limited to 15%. Must be licensed as a private investigator in Maine. §1976

Maryland

Comptroller of Maryland
Unclaimed Property Unit
301 W. Preston St.
Baltimore, MD 21201-2385
(410) 767-1700
(800) 782-7383
Call to have listings less than $100 searched.
Updated: At least once a month
Finders: Listing must have been in state custody for at least 24 months.

Massachusetts

Department of the State Treasurer
Abandoned Property Division
One Ashburton Place, 12th Floor
Boston, MA 02108-1608

(617) 367-0400
(800) 647-2300
Updated: Daily
Finders: Fees limited to 10%. Must be registered with the Abandoned Property Division. Finders may not also represent holders doing pre-escheat work. Listing must have been on the state site for 24 months.

Michigan

Department of the Treasury
Unclaimed Property Division
P.O. Box 30756
Lansing, MI 48909
(517) 636-5320
Updated: Monthly
Finders: No limit on fees. May need to be licensed as a private investigator in order to lawfully conduct investigations with respect to finding owners of unclaimed property.

Minnesota

Department of Commerce
Unclaimed Property Program
85 7th Place East, Suite 500
St. Paul, MN 55101-2198
(651) 296-2568
(800) 925-5668
Updated weekly on Tuesday
Finders: Fee limited to 10%. This amount can be exceeded if the document you signed contains a full disclosure. Call for details. Must be registered as a private investigator. Listing must have been in state possession for 24 months.

Mississippi
Mississippi Treasury
Unclaimed Property Division
P.O. Box 138
Jackson, MS 39205
(601) 359-3600
Updated: Nightly
Finders: Fee limited to 10%. Treasurer reviews all contracts. Listing must be in state possession at least seven months.

Missouri
State Treasurer's Office
Unclaimed Property Section
P.O. Box 1004
Jefferson City, MO 65102-1004
(573) 751-0123
Updated: Nightly, Monday-Friday
Finders: Property in state possession for:
More than 12 months but less than 24 months are limited to 10%;
More than 24 months but less than 36 months are limited to 15%;
More than 36 months is limited to 20%.
Finders must register with the State Treasurer and certify compliance and good standing with the tax, business registration and all other regulatory requirements as required in Missouri. To remain certified, the person must annually recertify compliance with such requirements. Property must be in state possession at least 12 months. (Statute 447.581)

Montana
Department of Revenue
Attn: Unclaimed Property
P.O. Box 5805
Helena, MT 59604-5805
(406) 444.6900
(866) 859-2254
Updated: Annually
Finders: Any fee above 15% is considered unconscionable.

Nebraska
Office of the State Treasurer
Unclaimed Property Division
809 P St.
Lincoln, NE 68508
(402) 471-8497
(877) 572-9688
Updated: Daily
Finders: Fees limited to 10%. Listing must have been in state possession for at least 24 months. 69-1317

Nevada
Office of the State Treasurer
Unclaimed Property Division
555 E. Washington Ave, Suite 4200
Las Vegas, NV 89101-1070
(702) 486-4140
(800) 521-0019
Updated: Nightly
Finders: Fees are limited to 10%. May be required to be licensed as private investigator.

New Hampshire
Treasury Department
Unclaimed Property Division
25 Capitol St. Room 121
Concord, NH 03301
(603) 271-2619
(800) 791-0920
Processing fee of $20 for liquidation or re-registration of securities
Updated: Monthly
Finders: Listing must be in state possession for at least 24 months.

New Jersey
Office of the State Treasurer
Unclaimed Property
P.O. Box 214
Trenton, NJ 08695-0214
(609) 292-9200
Updated: Monthly
Finders: Fee not to exceed 20%, except if it is in the pre-escheat phase when 35% is allowed. Listing must be in state possession for at least 24 months. 46:30B-106

New Mexico
Taxation and Revenue Department
Unclaimed Property Division
P.O. Box 25123
Santa Fe, NM 67504-5123
(505) 476-1774
Updated: Weekly

Finders: Agreements are void and unenforceable if it was entered in from the date the property was presumed abandoned until 48 months after it was received by the unclaimed property administrator. 7-8A-25 NMSA 1978

New York
Office of the State Comptroller
Office of Unclaimed Funds
110 State Street, 8th floor
Albany, NY 12236
(518) 270-2200
(800) 221-9311
Updated: Weekly
Finders: Maximum fee is 15%

North Carolina
Unclaimed Property Office
PO Box 20431
Raleigh, NC 27619-0431
(919) 508-1000
Updated: Every Monday
Finders: Fee limited to $1,000 or 20%, whichever is less. Finders must be registered and pay an annual fee. May need private investigator license. Pre-escheat agreements are void and unenforceable. Must be in state possession for 24 months.

North Dakota
North Dakota Dept. of Trust Lands
Unclaimed Property Division
PO Box 5523
Bismark, ND 58506-5523

(701) 328-2800
Updated: As reports are received
Finders: Fee not to exceed 10%. Must be licensed as a private investigator. Listing must be in state possession for at least 24 months.

Ohio
Department of Commerce
Division of Unclaimed Funds
77 S. High St., 20th Floor
Columbus, OH 43215-6108
(877) 644-6823
Updated: Weekly
Finders: Fee is limited to 10%. Finders must have a Certificate of Registration. Listing must be in state possession for at least 24 months.

Oklahoma
Office of the State Treasurer
Unclaimed Property Division
2401 NW 23rd St, Suite #42
Oklahoma City, OK 73107
(405) 521-4273
Updated: Daily
Finders: Fee limited to 25%

Oregon
Department of State Lands
Unclaimed Property Section
775 Summer St. NE, Suite 100
Salem, OR 97301-1279

(503) 986-5200 ext. 65293#
Updated: Daily, Monday-Friday
Finders: Must be licensed as a private investigator. Information on unclaimed property accounts is confidential for 1 year prior to going to the state and for 2 years once it's been turned over to the state.

Pennsylvania
Pennsylvania Treasury
129 Finance Building
Harrisburg, PA 17120
(717) 787-2465
(800) 222-2046
Newspaper publication does not have to include listings less than $250.
Updated: "Often"
Finders: Fees limited to 15%. § 1301.11 (g)

Rhode Island
50 Service Ave,
Warwick, RI 02886
(401) 462-7676
Updated: Weekly
Finders: Must be in state possession at least 24 months. § 33-21.1-35

South Carolina
State Treasurer's Office
Unclaimed Property Program
PO Box 11778
Columbia, SC 29211

(803) 737-4771
Some listings go back to the 1940s
Updated: Weekly
Finders: Fees limited to 15%. Family Privacy Protection Act forbids information obtained from the state agencies to be used for commercial purposes. Listing must be with the state for at least 24 months.

South Dakota
Office of the State Treasurer
Unclaimed Property Program
500 E. Capitol Ave., Suite 212
Pierre, SD 57501-5070
(605) 773-3379
(866) 357-2547
Updated: Weekly
Finders: Fees limited to 25% unless you agree in writing to pay more. Agreements made between 1 year prior to going to the state and for 2 years once it's been turned over to the state are unenforceable. 43-41B-36

Tennessee
Treasury Department
Unclaimed Property Division
502 Deaderick St.
Nashville, TN 37243-0203
(615) 741-6499
Updated: Annually
Finders: Fees limited to 10% or $50, whichever is greater. Must be licensed as a private investigator. Signed contracts must be approved by the unclaimed property division.

Texas
Texas Comptroller of Public Accounts
Unclaimed Property Claims Section
PO Box 12046
Austin, TX 78711-2046
(512) 463-3120
(800) 654-FIND (3463)
Updated: Nightly, except Saturday
Finders: Fees limited to 10%. Must be licensed through the
Texas Dept. of Public Safety, Private Security Bureau and hold
a current sales tax permit.

Utah
Treasurer's Office
Unclaimed Property Division
PO Box 140530
Salt Lake City, UT 84114
(801) 715-3300
(888) 217-1203
Updated: Daily
Finders: Listing must be in state possession for at least 24
months. 67-4a-705

Vermont
Office of the State Treasurer
Unclaimed Property
109 State St. 4th Floor
Montpelier, VT 05609-6200
(802) 828-2301, press 2
(800) 642-3191 (VT only)
TTY (800) 253-0191

Updated: Daily
Finders: Fee limited to 10%. Must register with the Treasurer's office and post a $10,000 bond. Listing must be in state possession for at least 24 months. § 1265

Virginia
Virginia Dept. of the Treasury
Division of Unclaimed Property
PO Box 2478
Richmond, VA 23218-2478
(804) 225-2142, press 1
(800) 468-1088
Updated: Weekly
Finders: Limited to 10%. Must have a valid business license in Virginia. Listing must be in state possession for 36 months.

Washington
Department of Revenue
Unclaimed Property Section
PO Box 47477
Olympia, WA 98504-7477
(360) 705-6706
(800) 435-2429 (WA only)
Updated: As reports come in
Finders: Fee limited to 5% and that's not just the state unclaimed property site. It includes 5 % for finding listings in cities, counties and other municipalities in regard to foreclosure proceeds. Finders must be registered with the state.

West Virginia
West Virginia State Treasurer's Office

1900 Kanahwa Blvd.
Capitol Complex Bldg #1, Room E-145
Charleston, WV 25305
(304) 558-5000
(800) 422-7498
Updated: Daily
Finders: Finders are not addressed in the WV Unclaimed
Property Act.

Wisconsin
Office of the State Treasurer
Unclaimed Property Unit
PO Box 2114
Madison, WI 53701-2114
(608) 267-7977
(877) 699-9211
Updated: Nightly
Finders: Fees limited to 20%. Must be in state possession at
least 12 months. Statute 177.35

Wyoming
Wyoming Unclaimed Property
2515 Warren Ave, Suite 502
Cheyenne, WY 82002
(307) 777-5590
Call if you want a "complete" search
Updated: Monthly
Finders: Agreements made between 1 year prior to going to the
state and for 2 years once it's been turned over to the state are
unenforceable. 34-24-136

US Territories
Guam
Treasurer of Guam
PO Box 884
Hagatna, GU 96932

Puerto Rico
Office of the Commissioner of Financial Institutions
Unclaimed Property, Salva D. Valentin
PO Box 11855
San Juan, PR 00910-3855
(787) 723-3130 ext 2330

Virgin Islands
Office of the L Governor
#18 Kongens Gade
St. Thomas, Virgin Islands 00802
(340) 774-7166

Canada
Alberta
Tax and Revenue Administration
Alberta Finance
9811-109 St.
Edmonton, AB T5K 215
(780) 427-3044

British Columbia
British Columbia Unclaimed Property Society
Box 12136 Harbour Centre
555 West Hastings St.
Vancouver, BC V6B 4N6
(604) 662-3518
(888) 662-2877
They have listings back to the late 1800s!
On the Web site, click Search for Unclaimed Property and then "Other Places to Look" for an extensive list of additional sites in Canada.

Ontario
Bank of Canada
Unclaimed Balance Services
234 Wellington St.
Ottawa, ON K1A 0G9
(800) 303-1282
Federally regulated bank or trust companies turn the money over to the Bank of Canada when the account is deemed dormant. Bank of Canada holds balances of $1,000 or more for 100 years. Balances of less than $1,000 are held for 40 years. As of

Dec, 2010 there were 1.3 million accounts worth $433 million, the oldest dating back to 1900.

Quebec
Direction principale des biens non réclamés
Revenu Québec
500, boulevard René-Lévesque Ouest, bureau 10.00
Montréal, Québec H2Z 1W7
(866) 840-6939
(800) 361-3795 Hearing Impaired

AFTERWORD

I hope you have found this information useful. I truly want to help you find your money.

I welcome your comments or additional information I may not have included or topics I didn't cover.

The ultimate compliment is your referral of people to my site.

From the bottom of my heart thanks to everyone who encouraged me and kept me focused starting with my mom, my son Ryan, my daughter-in-law Kelly; my esteemed nursing peers in the post anesthesia care unit at Indian River Medical Center who have stuck by me through multiple Ralph Kramden ideas especially Vicki Bottorf, who first told me about the missing money sites, Ann Sinoply, Marilyn Olavarria, and Donna Kreger; Linda Ulrich for her inspiration; Dr. Frazier for his generous support in my idea and my ability to achieve it as well as his financial support, plus his referral of Carol Bassett—my Editor (Thank you, Carol!); the faculty at Poynter who really taught me how to write during those amazing six weeks in 2001; and Steve and Bill Harrison for their Quantum Leap program—the single best program a wanna-be author could ever hope for.

I especially want to thank Suze Orman for the opportunity of a lifetime and Elisabeth Leamy from Good Morning America for all she does to help people find their missing money.

And finally, I hope the unclaimed property administrators will take steps to correct some of the problems with how the names are entered, as I have illustrated in the search tips. Go ahead. Make my book obsolete because you fixed all the problems. I'm OK with that.

It's all about people being able to find their money.

Happy treasure hunting!

Mary Pitman
